W9-CLW-623

GREAT ILLUSTRATED CLASSICS

A JOURNEY TO THE CENTER OF THE EARTH

Jules Verne

adapted by
Howard J. Schwach

Illustrations by
Pablo Marcos Studio

BARONET
BOOKS

BARONET BOOKS, New York, New York

Copyright © 2009
Waldman Publishing Corp.
New York, NY 10028

BARONET BOOKS is a trademark of Waldman Publishing Corp., New York, N.Y.

For inquires email info@waldmanbooks.com

Please visit us at http://www.waldmanbooks.com

Printed in the United States of America

SPMIC90758

Contents

About the Author

Jules Verne was born in Nantes, France, in 1828. As a boy, he longed to travel to unknown worlds and at 12, he tried to stow away on a ship bound for India. But his father pulled him off the ship and gave him a severe beating. Jules, however, vowed to continue to travel from then on—but only in his imagination.

While Jules Verne's imagination did not invent science fiction, Verne was the first writer to use actual settings for his science fiction stories.

Many people have said that Verne "invented

the future." They may be right, for Verne "invented" the submarine in *20,000 Leagues Under the Sea*, space travel in *From Earth to the Moon*, heavier-than-air flying machines in *The Clipper of the Clouds*, and around-the-world travel *in Around the World in 80 Days*.

But Verne was also fascinated with the past, and he takes his readers there in A *Journey to the Center of the Earth*. Verne first got the idea for the book at a dinner party, where he met two scientists who had just returned from exploring the volcanic island of Stromboli, off the coast of Italy. These two men had gone into a volcano's crater and then returned to the surface. But Verne's imagination was excited at the thought of *continuing* such a trip—right to the center of the earth itself!

The book you are about to read takes you on that very journey!

Professor Hardwigg

CHAPTER 1

The Great Discovery

Looking back at all that has happened to me since that eventful day, I am hardly able to believe that my adventures were real. They were so wonderful that, even now, I am amazed when I think about them.

I was living with my uncle, a German, who was a professor of philosophy, chemistry, geology, mineralogy, and many other "ologies."

Professor Hardwigg, my uncle, had invited me to study under him, for I was greatly interested in learning as much as I could about

7

the Earth and what lies under its surface.

Although my uncle was a most learned man, and could speak with the greats of the scientific world in almost any language, and could classify six hundred different geological specimens by their weight, hardness, sound, taste, and smell, he did not at all look the part.

He was fifty years old, tall, thin, and wiry. Large glasses hid his vast, round, bulging eyes. His nose was thin like a file and was constantly being attracted to tobacco. When he walked, he stepped a yard at a time, clenched his fists as if he were going to hit you, and then walked on. At most times, he was far from a pleasant companion.

But Professor Hardwigg is by no means a bad sort of man. However, to live with him means to obey him. So, when he came home one day and began to call, "Harry—Harry—Harry," I hastened to go at once, even though at the time I was more interested in finding out what was being prepared for dinner than

Hastening to the Professor's Call

what my uncle wanted from me.

I took the steps three at a time and presented myself to my uncle in his study. My uncle's study was a perfect museum, filled with minerals of every kind. When I entered, he was studying a book, not even aware that I had joined him in the room.

"Wonderful!" he said to himself as he studied the book. "Wonderful!"

The book was an old one, yellow with age—just the kind of book my uncle enjoyed the most.

"Did you want me for something, Uncle?" I asked.

"It is the *Heims-Kringla* of Snorre Tarleson," he said. "The famous Icelandic author of the twelfth century. It is a true account of the Norwegian princes who ruled Iceland."

"What language is it in?" I asked, hoping that it would be a German translation that I could read. But my uncle would have nothing

10

"Wonderful!"

of translations—only originals would do.

"It is a Runic manuscript," he said. "The language of the original population of Iceland." He was angry at my ignorance.

My uncle had picked up the book to show me the strange letters of this language, when a scrap of paper fell from between two of the yellowed pages.

My uncle siezed the paper like a hungry man snatching at a morsel of bread. It was an ancient parchment, about three inches by five inches, with strange-looking characters written all over it.

"It is Runic," my uncle declared, his voice and fingers trembling.

I looked at it closely. Little did I know then that this small parchment would lead us on one of the most wonderous adventures ever known to man.

But while my uncle could read Runic, he could not decipher the meaning of the letters on the parchment.

A Scrap of Paper Falls from the Pages.

Just then the cook called up to us that dinner was ready.

"I cannot be bothered with dinner!" my uncle yelled.

But I was hungry and went to dinner. I was just finishing the last of my dessert and wine when I heard my uncle roaring for me to come at once. I made a leap for the stairs to his study, so loud and fierce was his call.

My uncle was sitting, staring at the small piece of parchment. "I declare to you that it is Runic, "he yelled. "It contains some wonderful secret that I must get at, at any cost."

I looked at the letters on the parchment. They made no sense to my eye:

14

A Wonderful Secret on the Parchment

"Sit down!" my uncle cried fiercely. "And write what I tell you to write."

I obeyed at once.

"I will substitute a letter of our alphabet for that of the Runic," he said, "and we will see what that will produce."

He dictated the letters of these twenty-one words, none of which made any sense to me:

m.rnlls	*nicdrke*	*.nscrc*
sgtssmf	*Saodrrn*	*eeutul*
kt,samn	*emtnael*	*oseibo*
esruel	*Atvaar*	*rrilSa*
unteief	*ccdrmi*	*ieaabs*
atrateS	*dt, iac*	*frantu*
seecJde	*nuaect*	*Kediil*

Scarcely giving me time to finish taking them down, he snatched the paper from my hand and examined it with deep concentration. "I should like to know what it means," he said, as much to himself as to me.

16

"Write What I Tell You To Write."

But *I* certainly could not tell him.

"It reminds me of a cryptograph—a puzzle," he said. "I may be on the verge of a great discovery."

My opinion was that it was all rubbish, but I kept that opinion to myself, as my uncle's anger was not easy to bear.

"The parchment and the book are written in different hands," he said. "The book is about 200 years older than the parchment, so the parchment must have been written by some person who owned the book later than the original owner. So, the next question is, who owned this book?"

On the inside of the cover, my uncle found what at first looked like an ink stain, but on closer inspection, it proved to be a line of writing almost rubbed away by time. My uncle studied the letters:

Comparing the Parchment and the Book

"Arne Saknussemm!" my uncle cried in triumph. "He owned this book. He was a brilliant Icelandic professor and chemist of the sixteenth century. It was he who wrote the mysterious words on the parchment— perhaps some astounding discovery of his."

My uncle walked around the room in a state of excitement. "Until I discover the meaning of those words," he vowed, "I will neither eat nor sleep!"

"My dear uncle,..."I began.

"Nor will you either! " he cried.

I was glad that I had just eaten an unusually large meal.

My uncle and I tried various languages and variations of languages on the letters of the parchment. We worked for hours, but the parchment yielded no clue.

My uncle felt certain that Saknussemm had written his message in Latin, as most educated men of his time wrote. But the order of the letters provided no known Latin words.

Working for Hours on the Parchment

Then my uncle began reading the puzzling cryptograph all sorts of ways, according to some theory of his own, and he had me write the following:

mmessunkaSenrA.icefdoKsegnittamurt necertserrette,rotaiusadua,ednecsedsad- nelacartniiiluJsiratracSarbmutabeled- nek meretarcsilucoysleffenSnl.

It still made no sense to me. My uncle became enraged. He struck the table with his fist, then left the room and the house, slamming the doors behind him as he went.

I sat down for a while, relaxing and smoking. Then my mind returned to the parchment, and I picked it up and began studying it again. I found a few scattered Latin words, an English word, and several French words. It was enough to drive a man mad!

The heat in the closed room was too much to

The Professor Becomes Enraged!

bear, and I began to fan myself with the parchment. For the first time, I saw both the front and back of it.

Imagine my surprise when, glancing at the back of the parchment, I saw that the ink had gone through, revealing the Latin words *craterem*, "crater" and *terrestre*, "earth." I had discovered the secret! All I had to do to read the parchment was to look at it backwards.

My eyes were dazzled and my hands trembled with excitement as I began to read. But what horror and shock possessed me as I discovered the terrible secret! It had really been accomplished! A man had actually dared to do—what?

I immediately made a decision—no living being should know the parchment's secret.

"Never!" I cried. "Never will my uncle learn this dreadful secret!" He would immediately undertake the terrible journey revealed in the message. Nothing would stop him. I could not

24

Discovering the Terrible Secret!

allow such madness, nor could I take the chance of my uncle discovering the message. I would have to destroy it.

I snatched up the book and the parchment, and was about to toss them into the fire when my uncle entered the room. He did not even notice what I was about to do as he took the materials from me and began to look at them carefully. My flesh crawled as I realized that he might soon discover the way to read the parchment and its terrible secret.

Hours went by, but I dared not leave the room. I went to the sofa and soon fell asleep.

When I awoke, my uncle was still at work. His red eyes, matted hair, and feverish hands testified to his work. I loved him and truly felt sorry for his suffering, but I could not reveal the terrible secret.

He continued to study the parchment as night turned to morning, and morning turned to afternoon. At about two o'clock, he gave out a yell so loud that I almost fell from the sofa,

About To Toss Them into the Fire

where I was still resting.

"Backwards!" he cried. "It is backwards! Oh, how cunning Saknussemm was!" Then he began to translate the parchment:

"Descend into the crater of Yocul of Snefels, which the shade of Scartaris caresses, before the kadends of July, audacious traveler, and you will reach the center of the earth. I did it.

Arne Saknussemm"

My uncle leaped three feet off the ground, then ran about the room wildly, knocking over tables and chairs, and tossing his book up in the air. "We start at once! " he cried. "And you will share my glory."

"Start for where?" I asked, afraid of the answer.

"To the center of the earth!"

"Backwards! It Is Backwards!"

Studying a Map of Iceland

CHAPTER 2

Starting the Journey

It didn't take long for my uncle to take a book of maps from the shelf in order to explain Saknussemm's message to me.

"You see, the whole island is composed of volacanoes," he said as he pointed to a map of Iceland. "And they all bear the name *of Yocul,* which means glacier in Icelandic."

"But what does the word *Sneffels* mean?" I asked.

"I knew you would ask," my uncle answered. "Follow my finger to the western coast, past Iceland's capital, Reykjavik."

I followed his finger.

"There," he continued, "that peninsula shaped like a thighbone with a mountain in the center. Do you see it?"

I had to admit that I did.

"That is Sneffels," he said with some satisfaction. "It is a 5,000-foot-high mountain which shall be our doorway to the center of the earth."

"Impossible!" I cried.

"Why?" the professor asked.

"Because its crater is probably choked with lava, with burning rocks—and with many dangers."

"Suppose it is extinct?" he said. "That it has been dead for many years?"

"That *would* make a difference," I admitted. "But what is all this about *Scartaris* and the *Kalends* of July?"

"This shows how much Saknussemm knew about the area," my uncle answered. "The Sneffels Mountain has two peaks and many

32

"That Is Sneffels."

craters. Saknussemm is careful to point out the exact peak and crater. He lets us know that at the end of June, the sun is positioned in the heavens so that the shadow of Mount Scartaris, one of the peaks, falls upon only *one* crater. That is our highway to the center of the earth."

"But the theories about the heat...." I began.

"I care nothing for theories!" my uncle answered loudly. "Neither you nor anyone else really knows anything about the interior of the earth. The only way to learn its secrets is to go and see for ourselves."

I left the professor and went to see Gretchen, my uncle's god-daughter and the girl I hoped to marry. Though my uncle had warned me to say nothing about our adventure, I had to tell her.

"What a magnificent journey!" she said. "If only I were a man, I would go with you. It is a journey worthy of the nephew of Professor

Telling Gretchen about the Adventure

Hardwigg. Oh, Harry Lawson, I envy you."

I had expected that Gretchen would be against this mad journey, that she would beg me not to go. But her approval was the final blow.

I returned home to find my uncle in a state of great activity.

"Hurry and get packed!" he said. "You are wasting time."

"We are really going then?" I asked, hoping he would give the journey some more thought.

"We leave the day after tomorrow at daybreak," he answered.

We went by train from Hamburg, Germany, to Copenhagen, Denmark, and from there by schooner to Reyyavik, Iceland. The trip was a hard one, the seas rough and wild. We spent most of our eleven days at sea in our cabins, sick and pale. When we docked, my uncle was so haggard, he could scarcely climb to the deck.

When he stepped out on deck and looked

Sick at Sea for Eleven Days

around, however, his face brightened and he stood erect. He took my arm and held it tightly. "Behold!" he said, pointing to a high two-peaked mountain in the distance. "Behold the gateway to the center of the earth— Mount Sneffels!"

I smiled weakly, but said nothing.

"The worst difficulty is behind us," my uncle added as we left the ship and headed for our hotel.

"How is the worst difficulty behind us?" I asked with a cry.

"All we have to do now that we are here is to descend into the bowels of the earth," he answered matter-of-factly.

I would remember his answer many times in the days to come.

Later that night, we had dinner with a Mr. Fridriksson, one of Iceland's most learned scientists. We told him nothing of our planned journey, explaining only that we were here as tourists. However, we did learn from him more

The Gateway to the Center of the Earth

of the story of Arne Saknussemm. And what we learned made the reason for the coded parchment clear at last.

My uncle had asked Fridriksson if the library in Reykjavik had any books written by Saknussemm.

"You will not find any such books here in Iceland, nor anywhere else," the scientist said.

"Why not?" asked my uncle.

"Because Saknussemm was accused of heresy, of opposing the beliefs of the church, and in 1573 his books were all publicly burned .... But to turn to a more pleasant subject, Professor Hardwigg, I hope you find time during your visit here to examine some of Iceland's minerals. Some fine examples are to be found on Mount Sneffels."

"I might consider visiting there," said my uncle, barely hiding his delight.

"That will not be an easy trip, however," said Fridriksson. "There are no boats to take you across the bay. You will have to go by land

Saknussemm's Books Were Publicly Burned.

along the coast. But it is a very interesting route. To get there, you will need a guide, and I have just the man for you. I will bring him to your hotel tomorrow."

The following morning when I awoke, I heard my uncle's voice coming from the next room. I joined him and was introduced to a tall, strongly built man. His red hair was long, and his eyes were strong and intelligent. He seemed like a man who could be trusted.

His name was Hans Bjelke. Hans agreed to guide us to a village on the slope of Sneffels and remain in our service during my uncle's "scientific investigation." Little did Hans realize at that time that he would make history with us by accompanying us to the center of the earth!

We spent the next days getting our equipment together. Besides the normal climbing tools—pickaxes, crowbars, a ladder made of silk, iron-shod alpine poles, and strong rope, we took the following: a

Meeting Hans Bjelke, the Guide

thermometer which would read to 150É Centigrade (318ÉFahrenheit); a manometer to measure atmospheric pressure; a good watch; two compasses; a night glass; and two Ruhmkorff's lanterns and a battery to give us light. Our arms consisted of two rifles and two six shooters. I couldn't understand why we'd need them, for we had neither wild animals nor savage natives to fear. But I decided that my uncle had his reasons.

The weather was overcast but calm when we began our journey to Mount Sneffels.

"What do I risk?" I reasoned. "We will take a walk and climb a mountain and, if worst comes to worst, descend into the crater of an extinct volcano."

It took a full ten days to reach the foot of Mount Sneffels. My uncle and I rode horses; two more carried our equipment. But nothing could persuade Hans to climb on the back of any animal, so he made the trip on foot.

Along the way we had to cross small

Starting the Trip

mountains and large ones, and flatlands and fjords—those swirling bodies of water surrounded by rocky cliffs thousands of feet high. Hans led the way in such an easy manner that I began to believe that he could, indeed, lead us anywhere—even to the center of the earth.

We left the horses and began to climb Mount Sneffels in single file. Hans led the way along paths so narrow that two men could not pass. There was no time nor place for conversation, so we climbed in silence.

As we advanced, the road became difficult. Rocks broke under our feet and went rushing off the side of the mountain into the plains below. The cold was intense, and the wind blew violently. We had to avoid constant falls, yet Hans moved up the slope as if he were walking across a flat plain.

We spent the first night on the side of the crater, too excited to eat or sleep. But sleep finally did come, and the morning brought a

Climbing Mount Sneffels

surprise when we looked up. We were near the summit of one of Mount Sneffels' two peaks.

"What do you call this peak?" my uncle asked Hans.

"Scartaris," he replied, with the usual one-word answer that was his way.

A few more hours brought us to the summit and to the edge of the crater. I looked down into the inverted cone-shaped hole, half a mile wide, and thought, "To descend into this crater is like descending into the interior of a cannon, when it is loaded and ready to go off! This is the act of a madman!"... But I knew that I would soon do just that, and I felt like a lamb being led to slaughter.

We began our descent into the huge coneshaped crater, passing volcanic rocks and layers of deep, soft snow. We were tied to each other by a long rope to prevent accidents.

By midday, we were at the bottom of the crater, which was composed of three separate shafts. It was through these shafts that

Beginning the Descent into the Crater

Sneffels, when it was erupting, sent up its burning lava and poisonous vapors. My uncle ran to examine each of the three shafts, breathless with delight. Hans, seated on a pile of lava, looked at my uncle as if he were a lunatic.

Suddenly my uncle uttered a wild, unearthly cry. "Harry, Harry, come here quickly! This is wonderful! "

I ran to his side.

"Look there!" he cried, pointing at a rock wall.

I looked where he pointed. There, carved on the rock wall, was the name I had hoped never to see again—Arne Saknussemm!

"Look There!"

The Shadow Falls on the Central Shaft.

CHAPTER 3

Into the Bowels of the Earth

We waited two days for the overcast sky to open up and permit the sun to come out and cast the shadow of Scartaris on one of the three shafts. If it did not shine during these few days, we would have to put off our journey for an entire year.

Finally it happened. The sky cleared, and exactly at noon, the sun's rays sent the shadow of Scartaris on the central shaft.

"Here it is, " gasped my uncle joyously. "We have found it. Forward, my friends. Forward to the center of the earth! "

I looked at Hans to see his reaction to my uncle's words. But he only picked up his rope and calmly replied, "Forward."

Our real journey had now begun. We advanced to the mouth of the central shaft. It measured about a hundred feet in diameter. I stood on a rock at its edge and looked down.

The sides of the shaft went almost straight down, like the inside of a well, and ended in... nothingness! My hair stood on end, my teeth chattered, and my arms and legs grew weak. I felt like a drunken man.

We divided the food, equipment and instruments into three bundles, and each of us took a share on our backs. The clothes and ropes were tied into one bundle and tossed over the edge.

We began our descent with the aid of a rope wound around a large block of lava at the top. As we slid into the darkness, I realized that there were many natural footholds sticking out from the wall, which would help us in our

The Real Journey Begins.

downward climb. While I was concerned for our safety on the way down, my uncle was busy explaining to me the different layers of earth.

Soon we had reached a rock ledge. Hans pulled on one end of the rope. It unwound from the rock above and fell to his feet. We sat down to rest for a while on the ledge, then continued.

We climbed downward for three more hours. The bottom was not yet in sight, but a glance upward confirmed that the mouth of the crater was getting smaller and smaller as we got farther and farther away.

We had been climbing about ten and a half hours and had gone about 5,600 feet, or a mile into the earth, when a voice broke the silence.

"Halt!" cried Hans from the lead position.

"We have reached the end of our journey," my uncle said.

"What? The interior of the earth already?" I asked.

Resting on a Rock Ledge

"No, you stupid fellow!" he snapped. "But we have reached the bottom of the well."

"And we can go no farther?" I asked hopefully, looking forward to the upward climb.

"I can see a tunnel to the right," my uncle answered, dashing my hopes of leaving. "We will look at that tomorrow. Right now, let us eat and get whatever sleep we can."

Stretching out on beds of ropes and clothes, we did as he said.

At eight o'clock the next morning, a faint kind of dawn woke us. Light coming from the mouth of the crater sparkled from the prisms of lava on the crater wall, enabling us to see around us.

"Well, Harry," my uncle said, "did you ever pass a more comfortable night?"

"It *is* quiet here," I replied, "but there is something terrible in this calm. I'm still not sure we're doing the right thing."

"How can you be afraid, when we really

Sleeping on Beds of Rope and Clothes

haven't gone one inch into the bowels of the earth as yet?"

"What do you mean?" I asked, astonished.

"Look at the barometer," he said. "You will see that we have just about reached sea level Remember, we climbed up to enter the crater; and now we have gone just about as far down as we first climbed."

I checked the barometer, and he was, indeed, correct. We had just reached sea level.

My uncle took a small notebook from his pocket and began to write the first of the many notes he would keep

Monday, July 1st, 8:17.A.M.
Barometer, 29É Temperature, 43ÉFahrenheit. Direction, E.S.E.

The last observation referred to the direction of the tunnel we were to follow farther into the earth.

"Now, Harry, we are about to take our first steps into the bowels of the earth" my uncle said, "—bowels never before visited by man

60

Making the First of Many Notes

since the creation of the world."

With that, my uncle and Hans connected their batteries to the Ruhmkorf Coils hanging around their necks, and their lanterns immediately bathed the dark, gloomy tunnel in light.

"Forward!" cried my uncle, and we entered the tunnel, Hans first, then my uncle, and I third.

As I entered, I glanced up for a glimpse of light that was the Iceland sky. Little did I know then that I was never to see that sky again!

The great difficulty of our journey now really began. The way down was steeply inclined like a huge ramp. We were lucky that there were cracks and breaks in the rock and rocky soil that allowed us some footholds. Even though our equipment was heavy and the slope was steep, we moved rather easily, though slowly.

Many magnificent shades of lava from reds

Lanterns Bathe the Tunnel in Light.

to browns to yellows lined the tunnel. Crystals of quartz sparkled from the walls in our lights. To my surprise, we found no great increase in heat as we moved, or rather slid, slowly downward. Two hours after we entered the tunnel, the thermometer showed only 54É Fahrenheit—an increase of only 9 degrees.

About eight o'clock that evening, my uncle called a halt. The lamps were hung on the rock walls to provide light. We were in a large cavern. It was indeed beautiful, and I marveled at the beauty of the surroundings and the fact that there was plenty of air to breathe even at that depth.

We ate our dinner eagerly, but a feeling of uneasiness struck us all.

"We are halfway through our water supply, and we have not yet seen any springs of water," I said to my uncle. "And we have barely enough to last us five days."

"Be easy about that subject, Harry, and don't worry," my uncle said with a laugh. "We

Eating an Uneasy Dinner

will find plenty of water—in fact, more than we can use."

"But when?"

"When we get through this crust of lava. You cannot expect the water to force itself through these solid rock walls."

"If we keep moving horizontally, straight ahead, rather than vertically, straight down, we may never get through the crust," I said.

"What makes you think we are not going vertically?" my uncle asked, showing some surprise at my question.

"If we had been going straight down, far below sea level, the temperature would be up considerably," I said. "But it is not. It is only up 15 degrees, so I must conclude that we are not going far vertically. In fact, I would judge that we have gone no deeper than 1,125 feet."

The professor laughed. "Harry, my boy," he said, "would it surprise you to learn that, according to my calculations, we are at this moment at least 10,000 feet below sea level?"

"We Are 10,000 Feet Below Sea Level."

I was shocked. "How can that be? The temperature should then be 81 degrees."

The professor showed me his calculations and drawings. He was correct. So all the accepted scientific theories about the earth getting hotter as a person went deeper were, indeed, wrong as wrong can be!

Disproving Accepted Scientific Theories

Coming to the End of the Pathway

CHAPTER 4

Deeper and Deeper

The next day was Tuesday, the 2nd of July—and at six o'clock in the morning we resumed our downward journey. We followed the natural pathway made thousands of years ago by molten lava rising out of the earth. This pathway made for an easy descent because of its slope. After six hours of following the path, Hans stopped in his tracks. My uncle and I were soon at his side.

"We have come to the end of this pathway," my uncle said. And, indeed, he was right.

We were in the center of four small, narrow

tunnels which crossed each other in the shaft in which we stood.

"Which way do we go now?" I asked, hoping that the answer would be "back up."

But this was not to be. Without a moment's hesitation, my uncle pointed quietly to the eastern tunnel and, without delay, we entered its dark opening.

The descent in the tunnel was very gradual and twisting. Sometimes we walked through a series of arches such as might be found in a church—arches which seemed to soar high into the cave, lost to sight. Other times we had to crawl through a series of low, narrow tunnels that might have been made by some animal digging its way through the earth.

We walked, we slid, we clambered over piles of rocks, and we rolled down heaps of lava.

At six o'clock in the evening, after a tough day of climbing, we had gone about six miles southward, but less than a mile down. We ate in silence, rolled ourselves in our sleeping

Crawling Through Low, Narrow Tunnels

rugs, and fell quickly asleep soon afterwards.

After a night's sleep, we awoke fresh and ready for whatever adventures might await us on the new day.

The tunnel through which we were traveling soon became absolutely horizontal and, at times, even seemed to be sloping upward. Finding this upward climb tiring, I stopped, and my uncle, seeing this, came to me.

"What is the matter?" he asked. "Are you tired after only three hours?"

"Haven't you noticed that we are going not down, but up?" I asked him.

He looked shocked. "Up! How can that be?" he asked, looking at the sloping tunnel.

"There is no doubt about it," I said. "For the last half-hour, the slope has been upward. If we continue this way, we might find ourselves back in Iceland."

My uncle shook his head, not yet ready to admit that he had been mistaken by choosing the eastern tunnel. He would not answer me,

Going *Up*, Not Down!

but started once again moving along the upward tunnel, Hans first, then my uncle, then me. I did not want to lose sight of them. My worst fear was finding myself alone in this underground world. And, besides, I reasoned, each step now took us closer to the surface. That, in itself, was a good thing.

At about twelve o'clock I began to notice a change in the composition of the walls. They were no longer made solely of lava, but of living rock. I walked to one of the walls for a closer look.

"What's the matter now?" my uncle called, seeing me at the wall.

"Don't you see the different layers of calcium rock and the first indication of slate strata?" I asked.

"Well?" he said, as if waiting for a lecture.

"We have arrived at that period in the history of the world when the first plants and the first animals made their appearance on earth," I announced.

The First Plants and Animals on Earth

The professor never spoke a word. He took a look at the wall, then continued on ahead, leaving me disheartened.

"If we have left the lava walls behind, then we are *not* on our way back up to Mount Sneffels," I muttered to myself. "And if I am right, I should find some remains of these primitive plants and animals."

I began to search for these clues of the past. My feet, so long accustomed to the hard lava soil, found themselves walking on a kind of soft dust—the remains of plants and shells.

I stooped and picked up an almost perfect; shell, and ran to catch up to my uncle. "Do you see this?" I asked him.

"So?" he said. "You have found the shell of an extinct crustaceous animal, much like our present lobster, nothing more."

"Well...." I began.

"I know," he said. "We have left the lava tunnel, and it is possible that my choice of tunnels was wrong. But we shall have to go to

Finding the Shell of an Ancient Lobster

the end of this one to see for sure."

And on he went.

We had not yet found any water, and we forced ourselves to go on rations. Our supply would certainly not last more than three days. I had read of the horrors of thirst, and I knew that, being where we were, it would mean the swift end of our journey... *and our lives!*

During the whole next day, we made our way through this never-ending tunnel. We no longer spoke to each other; we just walked quietly along. Sometimes the road still moved slightly upward, but more usually, it had a downward slant.

We saw many other remains of old plants and animals as we climbed. The strata never changed, and I began to hope that either one of two things would happen: one, that we'd reach a deep well and be able to go straight downward, or two, that we'd hit a blank rock wall and have to go back the way we came.

But when evening came, neither of those

Going on Water Rations

two possibilities had been realized.

On Friday, after a night in which I felt a real thirst for the first time, we again began our journey. After about ten hours of slow movement through a series of tunnels, the reflection of our lights off the tunnel walls grew dimmer and dimmer. At first, I thought that our lamps were going out. But when I placed my hand against a wall, my fingers came away pitch black.

"A coal mine!" I loudly exclaimed.

"A coal mine without miners," my uncle answered back quickly.

We stopped at that point for supper, but I was so thirsty that I could hardly eat. I sat and waited for the few drops of water that were my evening's ration. The others fell asleep, but I could not. I lay in my sleeping rug, counting the hours until morning.

At six o'clock we resumed our journey through the coal mine, and twenty minutes later we came upon a huge tunnel. It was

Pitch-Black Fingers

about a hundred feet wide by a hundred fifty feet high—a natural cavern cast apart by some underground disturbance thousands of years before.

As I gazed at the wonderous cavern made up of vast layers of coal, an uneasiness fell over me. What was bothering me? ... Then suddenly I knew! My nose had detected an odor of gas. The cavern was filled with a dangerous gas, which coal miners call "fire damp." One spark could set off an explosion that would kill all of us instantly. Luckily, we lit our way with battery lanterns and not flaming torches, or we would all now be dead.

We left the cavern and continued on our way along the dark tunnel. It was so dark that we could not see more than a few feet ahead. My uncle was impatient for the road to cease its horizontal direction and start heading downward. I felt that the tunnel would go on this way for months.

Suddenly, at six o'clock, we came face to face

Dangerous Fire Damp Gas!

with a blank wall. To the left, to the right, above, and below, there was no place to go. We were at a dead end! We stood and stared at the wall, wondering what to do next.

Finally, my uncle spoke. "Well, so much the better," he said. "At least we know we are not on the road taken by Arne Saknussemm. All we have to do is go back. Let us rest tonight, and within three days we shall be back at the point where the four tunnels began."

"If our strength lasts that long," I said with some bitterness. "Tomorrow, there will not be a drop of water left. It is almost gone."

" And your courage with it?" my uncle asked in a severe tone.

What could I say? I turned around and fell asleep, dreaming of water. I would have gladly traded a diamond mine for one glass of cool spring water.

A Blank Wall—and No Place To Go!

Suffering on the Way Back

CHAPTER 5

Where Is the Water?

The next day, our departure took place at a very early hour. There was no time for even the least delay. According to my figures, it would take us five days to get back to the place where the tunnels divided.

I can never describe all the suffering we endured on the way back. My uncle accepted the suffering in silence, finally convinced that he had made a great error by choosing the eastern tunnel. Hans, that strong man, accepted all that came his way with quiet strength. As for myself, well, I must admit that I did nothing but complain about the terrible situation we were in.

As I had expected, our supply of water gave out completely on the first day's march. I was so tired that more than once I came close to collapsing on the rocky ground.

When this finally did happen, Hans and my uncle stopped and tried to comfort me. But I could see that fatigue and lack of water were torturing my uncle as well.

After a time, I moved along without thinking or feeling. I remember nothing of this period of time except that it was like a horrible nightmare.

At last, at ten o'clock in the morning, on Tuesday, the 8th of July, after crawling on our hands and knees for many hours, more dead than alive, we reached the point where the eastern tunnel began.

I lay like a dog, on the hard, dry lava, unable to rise. Deep groans and sighs passed from my lips, then I fell into a faint.

Soon, I felt my uncle lift me tenderly in his

Lying on the Hard, Dry Lava

arms. Through the fog that had enveloped my mind, I heard him tearfully say, "Poor boy!"

I tried to speak, but I could not. I squeezed his trembling hand to show him that I was all right. He reached to the ground and brought up his drinking gourd, then put it to my lips.

"Drink, my poor boy, drink," he said.

Had I heard right? Was my uncle mad? Yet before I could ask myself those questions a second time, a mouthful of water cooled my parched lips and throat.

"One mouthful of water, the very last," my uncle said. "I've saved it at the bottom of my bottle for you. Twenty times, a hundred times, I've resisted the temptation to drink it. I knew that when we reached this point, you would need it to go on."

"Thank you, my dear uncle," I cried. "Thank you from the bottom of my heart." And big tears rolled down my feverish cheeks.

My uncle smiled kindly at me.

"Well," I said, "there is little doubt about

The Very Last Mouthful of Water

what we must now do. There is no more water, therefore our journey is at an end. Let us return to Sneffels."

"Go back?" my uncle said, speaking more to himself than to anyone else. "Must it be that way?"

"Yes!" I cried. "Go back—and now. We haven't a moment to lose."

"So, my dear Harry," the professor said after a moment's silence, "those few drops of water have not brought back your energy or your courage?"

I couldn't believe what I was hearing. "Aren't *you* discouraged, sir?" I asked.

"What!" he bellowed. "Give up just when we are on the verge of success? Never! Never shall it be said that Professor Hardwigg gave up!"

"Then we must make up our minds to die," I said quietly.

"No," my uncle answered. "Go, go back and take Hans with you. I will go on alone."

"Give Up? Never!"

"You ask us to leave you?"

"Leave me, I say. I will complete this journey, or I will never return to the surface of the earth. Now go."

I couldn't believe what my uncle was saying. I went to Hans, who sat quietly watching the scene between my uncle and myself. I caught his hand in mine, but he never moved a muscle. I pointed the way up, the way to the summit of Mount Sneffels.

The Icelander gently shook his head and pointed to my uncle. "Master," he said quietly.

"The master is a madman!" I cried. "We must drag him with us. Do you hear me?"

Although I tugged furiously at his arm, Hans did not move an inch.

Then my uncle spoke, quietly yet firmly enough to get my instant attention. "My good Harry, be calm," he said. "Listen to what I have to say to you."

I sat back then, folded my arms, and looked

Appealing to Hans for Help

my uncle squarely in the eye.

"The lack of water is the sole obstacle to the success of our journey," he said. "In all of our travels we have found no water. However, while you were unconscious, I explored the entrances to the other three tunnels, and I found that one goes directly downwards into the bowels of the earth. If we follow that one, it will take us directly to the layer of rock that is guaranteed to have springs. We shall have all the water we need in a few hours."

I said nothing.

"One more day—that is all I ask," he added. "If we find no water within that time, I will give up this journey, and we will all return to the surface."

I knew how much this journey meant to my uncle and how great a chance he was taking by making this offer. So I had to agree to the one day. "Let us go then," I said. "One day, and we then return to the surface where we belong."

The Professor Pleads for One More Day.

We now began our second descent—this one into the western shaft. The tunnel we entered and traveled along was a fissure in the earth, probably caused when the hot earth began to cool at the beginning of its life. For a geologist, this was a paradise of rock specimens never before seen by man. I could have spent days just looking and touching the many rock formations, with threads of copper, manganese, platinum, and gold running through them.

It was now eight o'clock, and we still had not found any water. The sufferings I endured were horrible, but my ears were alert to catch the sound of a spring. I listened and listened, but never did I hear a drop.

Suddenly, I felt a deadly faint come over me. My legs refused to support me any longer. My eyes could not see. I gave one despairing cry and began to fall forward. "Help, help, I'm dying!" I cried.

Just before my eyes closed, I saw my uncle

Listening for the Sound of a Spring

standing over me, his face tortured with pain and sorrow. "All is over," he said quietly.

When I opened my eyes again, I saw my uncle and Hans lying near me, wrapped in their sleeping rugs. Were they asleep or dead? I could not think of sleeping. All I could think of was the miles and miles of the earth's crust above me, weighing on me like some giant cloak...crushing me in my granite bed.

I lay there for hours. The silence was like a tomb. Suddenly, a movement caught my eye. Hans was moving away from our camp with a lamp in his hand.

"Hans is leaving us," I cried. "Hans— Hans, if you are a man, come back!"

Then I realized that those words were spoken only to myself. I was immediately ashamed of my suspicions. Hans was going down deeper into the tunnel, not up. He must be searching for the water that would save us. Had he, in the silence of the earth, heard the sound of a spring?

"Hans, Come Back!"

Hans Returns.

CHAPTER 6

The Hansbach

When Hans didn't return in the next hour, wild reasons why he would have left us crossed my mind, each reason crazier than the last. I must have been either half or wholly mad.

Suddenly, I heard the sound of footsteps coming up the tunnel and saw Hans's light shining on the walls of the passage.

Hans approached my uncle and gently wakened him.

My uncle instantly rose and asked, "Well?"

"Water," said Hans, without a trace of emotion.

"Water, water!" I cried wildly, clapping my hands and jumping up and down.

"Where?" asked my uncle.

"Below."

We quickly got ready to move, and within a short time we were making a rapid descent into the tunnel.

An hour later, we had advanced a thousand yards and had descended two thousand feet. At that moment, I heard a familiar sound—a kind of dull roar, like that of a distant waterfall.

"Hans was right," my uncle cried happily. "That is the roar of moving water."

"There can be no doubt?" I asked, still afraid to be certain.

"There's not the slightest doubt about it," my uncle answered. "An underground river is running beside us somewhere."

At first it sounded like the river ran right above our heads, then the sound came from the wall at our left. I touched the hard rock

"Water, Water!"

wall, hoping to find a sign of moisture or of the coolness of the water. But all I could feel was the hard rock itself.

We advanced down the tunnel. A half-hour passed, then an hour. We could hear the water, but it was so deeply buried in the hard rock that we could not touch or see it.

We continued to walk, but the sound of the water seemed to be getting dimmer. It was obvious that we were moving away from the water, so we retraced our steps to the point where we could hear the water the loudest. There, we stood silently and stared at the wall.

In a few moments, a smile broke across Hans' face. He went to the wall, put his ear against it, and smiled again. Then he picked up a crowbar and began attacking the wall three feet above the tunnel floor.

"Saved!" I cried. "We're saved!"

"Yes," cried my uncle, even more excited than I. "Hans is right. We would never have thought of that ourselves."

Hans Attacks the Wall with a Crowbar.

After an hour's work with his crowbar, Hans had made a hole six inches wide and two feet deep into the rock. The hole could not be wider or else it would bring the entire wall down on Hans—and on us.

The waiting was terrible. I could taste the water so much that my lips and throat became even more parched than before.

My uncle and I were just getting ready to go to work on the wall ourselves, whatever the danger, when we heard a loud, welcome hiss. Then a jet of water burst through the wall with such force that it hit the opposite side of the tunnel.

Hans cried out in pain. I did not understand why, until I plunged my hands into the sparkling water and drew back with a wild, frantic cry.

"It's boiling hot!" I cried in disappointment and pain.

"Well, never mind," my uncle answered. "It will soon cool."

A Jet of Water Bursts Through the Wall.

My uncle was right. In a short time, enough of the liquid was cool for each of us to have a long drink. We drank greedily, without really tasting the water at all. Afterwards, I realized that the water had a mineral taste to it

"Since we are the first travelers to discover the stream," said my uncle, "I think we should name it after Hans."

"Agreed," I said.

We named the stream *Hansbach,* or Hans's stream.

I wanted to fill our goatskins with the precious liquid, but my uncle explained that the flowing water would follow us in our descent and provide refreshment when we needed it.

"Then there is no reason why we cannot now continue on our journey, " I said.

"Ah, my boy," my uncle said, laughing, "you have finally begun to believe that the journey is possible."

"Not only possible, sir," I said, "but I am

Drinking Greedily

now confident of our success. Let us get on with our descent."

But my uncle was not ready. "Just a, moment," he said. "It is night, and we ought to sleep for a while before we continue."

By the next day, Thursday, when we awoke, I had forgotten all our past suffering. We had a good breakfast, drank our fill of the water that had been cooling all night long, and began our descent at eight o'clock in the morning.

The tunnel moved downwards in twists and turns to the southwest, according to my; uncle's compass. That day and the next, we did a considerable amount of horizontal, but very little vertical, traveling, although at times the way did get steep.

On Friday evening, the 10th of July, we estimated our position to be ninety miles southeast of Reykjavik, Iceland, and about seven and a half miles deep into the earth. We now received a startling surprise.

Under our feet there opened a deep well. It

The Tunnel Moves Downwards.

went straight down into the earth and was frightening to look at.

But my uncle did not think so. "Look at this!" he cried with delight. "The rock projections in this well will serve as a staircase to take us a long way into the bowels of the earth."

Hans-got out the ropes, and we began our descent into the well. We were, in fact, descending a narrow spiral, much like the staircase found in some homes. As trained geologists, we had done climbing such as this before, and once we began the descent, it did not seem too bad an idea at all.

After a while, however, our calves ached, and we had to stop to rest every fifteen minutes. We ate and drank as we rested, for the water from the Hansbach flowed down the well along with us.

During the next two days, Saturday and Sunday, we followed this spiral staircase downward, going about six miles farther into

Following a Spiral Staircase Downward

the earth. We were now about 15 miles below sea level.

On Monday, however, at about noon, the well took a more gentle slope, and we were traveling more on a road.

We traveled that road until Wednesday, the 15th, when we were actually 21 miles below sea level. My uncle calculated that we were approximately 150 miles from Sneffels, where we had begun our journey fifteen days before.

"If your calculations are right, Uncle," I said, "we are no longer under Iceland."

"Do you think so?" he asked.

"We can easily find out," I said, pulling out a map and compasses.

I measured carefully, then held a map out to my uncle. "You see," I said, "those 150 miles to the southeast put us under the open sea."

"Under the open sea!" cried my uncle with delight.

"No doubt," I said. "The ocean flows over our heads this very minute."

Measuring Their Location

This idea was not such a pleasant one to me—the mighty Atlantic Ocean was resting on the granite roof above my head!

Three days later, Saturday, the 18th of July, we reached a vast grotto—a kind of underground cavern. My uncle decided that the next day being Sunday, we should have a day of rest.

Reaching a Vast Grotto

Breakfast in the Grotto

CHAPTER 7

Alone and Lost!

I awoke on Sunday morning without any sense of hurry, not concerned with starting another day's travel.

The grotto we were in was a vast and magnificent hall. The Hansbach flowed slowly along the grotto's granite floor. The water was now so far from its fiery source that it was cool enough to drink without waiting.

After breakfast, my uncle went to work putting his notes in order. "Upon our return to the upper regions, I want to make a map of our journey," he said. "The map will be a cross-section of the earth, as discovered in our journey."

"Do you think you can do that accurately?" I asked.

"I have been keeping charts of the direction and angle of our travel," he answered. "I am sure I made no mistakes. We have traveled 250 miles from the point of our departure."

He looked down at his notes and made some more calculations. Then he added, "And, we have gone almost 50 miles in a downward direction."

"Fifty miles!" I cried. "That is the entire thickness of the earth's crust, according to scientists."

"I don't deny that," my uncle said.

"Then, at this depth," I added, "according to all scientific laws, the temperature should be 1500 degrees!"

"*Should* be," said my uncle. "But you see my boy, that it is not so, for if it *were* 1500 degrees, these granite rocks would be melted.

The Professor Makes More Calculations.

So you see, as is usually the case, facts are overruling scientific theories."

"I agree," I said, "but I am nevertheless surprised, for the actual temperature here is 27.6 degrees. Let me then draw a conclusion from these facts."

"Go ahead," said my uncle.

"Let us say that from where we are now, the depth from the surface to the center of the earth is about 4,800 miles," I began.

"That's correct," my uncle said.

"And," I continued, "we have traveled about 50 of those 4,800 miles. And we have taken twenty days to do it."

"Yes, yes," he said. "Go on."

"If we go on this way, traveling more horizontally than vertically," I concluded, "it will take us about five and a half years to get to the center of the earth! "

My uncle had an objection. "How do you know that this tunnel does not go straight into the earth without any of the horizontal

126

Drawing a Conclusion from the Facts

movement that cost us so much time earlier?"

I had no answer.

"And," he added, "you forget another thing. Another man has successfully completed the trip. Why should he have succeeded if we are doomed to failure?"

Again, I had no answer, but I did have an objection. In the sixteenth century, when Arne Saknussemm had made his journey, neither the manometer nor the barometer had yet been discovered. How, then, did he know that he had indeed reached the *center* of the earth? I thought about this, but I did not voice an objection to my uncle. It would only have served to make him angry. So I decided to agree with him and follow him to whatever destiny he chose to lead me. After all, I had to admit that things had actually been going rather well and that the goal was worth the hardships we had so far endured.

During the next two weeks after that Sunday's rest, the slopes became steeper and

Did Saknussemm Reach the *Center*?

more frightening. Some, in fact, were almost vertical, and we had to descend them with the use of ropes. But we made rapid progress, covering on some of those days five or six miles in our downward journey towards the center of the earth.

During those weeks, nothing of interest happened. But the next event that took place will remain in my memory forever. It is so terrible, in fact, that even now as I think about it, my soul shudders and my blood runs cold.

It happened on the 7th of August. We were about 600 miles southeast of Iceland. Our continuous descent had taken us 90 miles into the bowels of the earth. Above our heads were nearly 100 miles of rocks, oceans, continents, towns, and living beings.

On that memorable day, the tunnel had taken a nearly horizontal course. I had the lead and was carrying one of the lanterns. My uncle was second with another lantern, and Hans was trailing behind.

The Tunnel Takes a Horizontal Course.

I was busy examining the different layers of granite rock along the way and so completely absorbed in my work that I paid no attention to anything else. Suddenly, I stopped and turned around to say something to my uncle and found that...I was alone!

"Well," I thought to myself, "I must have been walking too fast. Or perhaps my uncle and Hans have stopped to rest. The best thing I can do is to go back and find them."

So I retraced my steps for about fifteen minutes. Rather uneasily, I paused and looked eagerly around. There was nobody in sight.

I called out as loudly as possible, "Uncle! Hans!"

The only response was the echo of my voice as it bounced off those terrible rock walls. A cold shiver shook my body, and perspiration burst out upon my skin.

"I must be calm", I said aloud in an effort to drive away my fears. "I'm sure that I will find them. There cannot be two roads. I must go

"Uncle! Hans!"

farther back down the tunnel."

I walked back through the tunnel for another half an hour. There was still no sign of either my uncle or Hans. My calls brought only the echo of my own words.

At last I stopped. It was hard to realize that I was alone—that I had made a mistake and was lost. "Come, come," I said to myself "There is only one road, and we must meet soon." But my voice no longer sounded convincing, even to my own ear.

There was no reason to panic. I still had the Hansbach. I would follow my faithful river back up the tunnel and find my way out if I had to. I stooped to plunge my hands into the pleasant waters of my little stream ... but my hands hit only a hard, dusty road of granite. With horror, I realized that the stream I had been counting on to save me ... had completely disappeared!

The Hansbach . . . Has Disappeared!

Buried Alive, Alone!

CHAPTER 8

Voices At Last!

No words in any language can describe my utter horror. I was buried alive, alone, 100 miles inside the earth, with nothing to look forward to except death—the slow, horrible death brought on by hunger and thirst.

I crawled about, feeling the dry, hard rock. "How did I lose the course of the stream?" I asked myself over and over.

It was now clear that when we stopped a while back, the water of the Hansbach must have flowed into another tunnel, while I, unknowingly, had taken a different path. To what depths had my uncle and Hans gone? Had they gone forward—or back?

"Lost! Lost! Lost!" I cried out.

And the walls echoed my words back to my ears like a cruel reminder of my fate.

I was lost at a depth which, to my wild mind, appeared to be without measure. Those 100 miles of the crust of the earth above me weighed upon my shoulders so heavily that I felt myself crushed by the awful weight. It was indeed a position to drive the sanest man to madness!

"Oh, Uncle!" was my tortured cry. "Oh, dear Gretchen! Will I ever see you again?"

When I realized that no further aid could expected from man, and knowing that I, myself, could do no more for my own rescue, I asked assistance from Heaven. I prayed.

This prayer brought me a certain measure of calm, and I began to take an intelligent look the situation I was in.

I had about three days' food with me, and

Asking Assistance from Heaven

my water bottle was full. But one fact remained clear—I had to find my companions. But which course should I take? Should I go up or down?... I finally decided that it was best to retrace my steps in upward direction.

By doing this carefully, I hoped to reach the point where I had left the stream and entered the wrong tunnel. There, I would surely find the rippling Hansbach again and, if need be, the pathway to the surface.

After a slight meal, I began my upward journey. I looked at the projections of rocks I passed, hoping to see familiar signs.

But I was soon forced to admit that the path would never take me back to where I had lost my uncle and Hans. The path I was climbing led me to... a solid wall of rock! I could go neither left nor right nor up.

I collapsed on the hard granite floor. My last hope was gone. I would never find the Hansbach or my uncle or Hans. I was doomed

The Last Hope Is Gone.

to die in this rock tomb. No words could describe my despair.

I tried to cry aloud, but only hoarse, animal-like sounds passed across my parched lips Then another horror possessed me. In falling down, I had damaged my lamp. Its light got dimmer and dimmer until, at last, with a final tremble, it went out—the last bit of light was ever destined to see!

A wild cry for help passed my lips. But there was no answer in return. Madness must have taken possession of me. I got up and began running downwards, screaming at the top of my lungs. I roared, I howled, I yelled. I crashed into pointed rocks along the walls. I fell over and over, and picked myself up, all covered with blood.

Hour after hour I ran this way, until at last having exhausted my strength, I fell into heavy mass on the side of a tunnel and lost consciousness!

When I came back to a sense of life at last, I

The Lamp Gets Dimmer.

found myself lying in a heap in the dark. Tears were running down my face, and blood was running from many parts of my body.... "Why wasn't I dead?" I wondered. And the realization that I was alive gave me some hope. Then, just as I was about to pass out again, my ears suddenly picked up a deep, rumbling sound coming from somewhere in the rock above me.

I listened carefully for many minutes, hoping to hear the sound again, hoping to discover its origin. An explosion of some gas? The fall of a rock?

Suddenly, my ear leaned against the wall accidentally, and I heard it again. It sounded like distant voices. "It cannot be!" I cried. "It must be a hallucination!"

I listened to the wall again. Yes, it *was* human voices. There was no doubt in my mind. The voices must belong to my uncle and Hans!

"Help!" I cried at the top of my voice. "Help, I am dying!"

Listening to Distant Voices

I listened for a response. But there was only silence. I began to fear that my weakened voice could not reach my companions.

"It must be them!" I cried. "What other men would be buried 100 miles under the earth?"

I crawled as close to the wall as I could get and, in my loudest voice, I called, "Uncle! Hans!"

Several seconds went by. They seemed like centuries.

Then, suddenly, these words reached my eager ears: "Harry, my boy, is that you?"

There was a short delay between question and answer.

"Yes—yes."

"Where are you?"

"Lost!"

"And your lamp?"

"Out."

"But the guiding stream—the Hansbach?"

"It is lost."

146

Harry Calls in His Loudest Voice.

"Keep up your courage, Harry. We will do our best to reach you."

"Don't leave me, Uncle!" I cried. "Keep speaking to me!"

"Keep up your courage!" my uncle answered. "We have been searching for you both upward and downward in this tunnel. I feared we had lost you forever. I had begun to give up all hope. We are talking now because of some strange sound arrangement in the tunnels. We may actually be far apart, but our voices are traveling along the tunnel walls. But do not fear, my boy, we will find you."

"Uncle," I said, my heart beating madly, "we should try to find out how far apart we are.

"Yes, of course," he called.

"Do you have your watch at hand?" I asked.

" I do, " he answered.

"Take it in your hand and call my name. Be sure to note the exact second you speak. I will answer you as soon as I hear your voice. Then

"Keep Up Your Courage!"

note the exact second that my voice reaches you."

"Very good," he said. "I will record the time it takes for my sound to reach you and return, and I shall figure out the distance between us. I am ready to say your name now."

I put my ear to the wall. As soon as I heard the word "Harry" come to my ear, I repeated it to the wall. Then I waited.

"Forty seconds," called my uncle. "It took forty seconds. Twenty seconds each way. Now, figuring that sound travels 1,020 feet each second, we get 20,400 feet—about five miles."

The words fell on me like a death song. "Five miles," I muttered in despair.

"We shall get to you," my uncle called. "Have no fear."

"How do you know whether to go upwards' or downwards?" I asked.

"We must both descend," he answered. "We are in separate tunnels sloping downward into

Forty Seconds ... but Five Miles Apart!

a vast cavern. If you can walk, move in a downward direction, and we will surely meet."

Those words gave me some courage. I rose to my feet, but I could not walk. So I dragged myself along. The slope suddenly became very steep, and I was fearful of falling. I clutched at the rock walls; I threw myself backwards. But it was in vain.

In an instant, I was dropping... dropping into a dark tunnel, almost a well. My head hit a rock, and I lost consciousness. As far as I was concerned, Death had claimed me for his own.

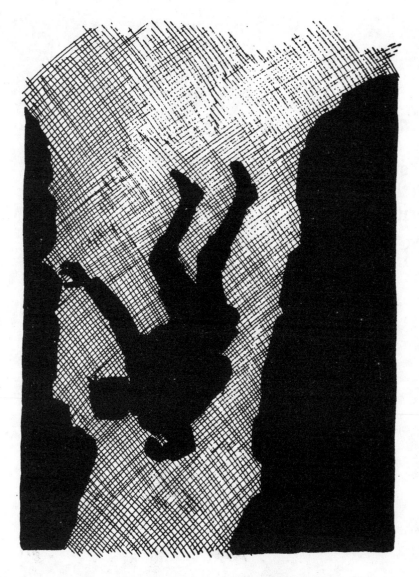

Dropping into a Dark Tunnel

Regaining Consciousness

CHAPTER 9

The Central Sea

When I regained consciousness, I found myself lying on some thick sleeping rugs. I groaned and opened my eyes to find my uncle gazing at me with tears in his eyes.

"He lives! He lives!" cried my uncle.

"Yes, my good uncle," I whispered.

At that point, Hans joined us. "Good day," he said.

"Where are we, Uncle?" I asked. "What day is this? What happened?"

"It is eleven o'clock at night on Sunday, August 9th," my uncle answered. "Your head

155

is bandaged and you need to sleep. I will tell you everything tomorrow."

As my eyes closed, I realized that my dangerous adventure in the interior of the earth in total darkness had lasted four days!

When I awoke the next day, I began to look around me. The cave floor was a soft, silvery sand, and the ceiling was adorned with magnificent stalactites glittering in all the colors of the rainbow. Though no torch lit the cave, light seemed to be coming from somewhere. I even imagined I could hear the sighing of the wind and the breaking of waves on a beach. Of course, all of that was impossible, for we were 100 miles below the surface.

Was I dreaming? Or had some great crack in the earth brought the wind and the sea to me? Or had my uncle given up his expedition and carried me back to the surface? I was puzzling over these questions when my uncle joined me.

"Good morning, Harry," he said. "You are looking better. Hans has treated your wounds

Is This a Dream?

with his own special ointment, and they are healing marvelously. Now, would you like to eat?"

For the ffrst time in days, I was hungry. And as I ate, my uncle explained that my fall had brought me down an almost vertical tunnel along with a rock slide right into his arms.

" It is indeed a miracle that you are alive," h said. "We must never separate again."

I looked at my uncle in astonishment—the journey, then, was not over. "But haven't we returned to the surface?" I asked.

"Certainly not," he replied.

"Then I must be mad, for I see daylight and hear the wind and the waves."

My uncle smiled. "You see and hear correctly," he said. "I cannot explain, but you must see for yourself."

"Let us go," I cried, eager to satisfy my curiosity.

"Just a moment. Do you feel well enough?

Seeing Daylight

After all, the wind is quite rough, and you must be strong for your sea voyage."

"My sea voyage?" I cried.

"You will see. You must be ready to go on board by tomorrow, and it may be a long trip."

Go on board *what* and *how?* My curiosity had to be satisified. So I rushed from the cave.

At first, I could not see anything because my eyes were not accustomed to the light, and I was forced to close them. When I reopened them, I stood stupified at the scene!

"The sea—the sea!" I cried.

"Yes," said my uncle. "The Central Sea, as I have named it."

It was quite true. The sea spread before me as far as my eyes could see. Its shore was made up of soft golden sand, sprinkled with shells. Waves broke on the shore with a murmur found only in underground places.

Back from the beach, huge rocky cliffs rose higher than my eyes could see. Above my head, gases formed thick clouds, partially

The Central Sea

concealing the granite roof that I knew was miles above my head. Yet from between these clouds shone an unusually beautiful ray of light—not like the sun, for it gave off no heat.

We were in some gigantic cavern, more wonderful than any I had ever read about. It left me speechless!

My uncle and I strolled along the beach breathing in the salt air after forty-seven days of dark tunnels. Beautiful waterfalls leaped down the rocky cliffs and disappeared into the sea.

After we had gone about 500 yards, we turned a sharp bend and found ourselves close to a huge forest. The trees, shaped almost like umbrellas, stood tall and motionless despite the strong breeze. I could identify most of the 2,000 known trees in the world, but I had never seen any quite like these before.

We went towards the forest. When at last we reached it, I found that I stood not in a forest of trees, but a forest of... *giant mushrooms*!

162

A Forest of . . . Giant Mushrooms!

The white mushrooms stood nearly forty feet high, with tops spreading forty feet across.

We walked on and found new wonders with every step: ferns as big as pine trees, giant grass, and trees as tall as a hundred feet in height.

"Astonishing! Magnificent!" cried my uncle. "These specimens, which are only small plants in our garden today, were all mighty trees when the world began!"

"If this is true of plant life, would it not also be true of animal life?" I asked, looking around anxiously.

"Yes, my boy. Just look at the bones up ahead on the beach—some as gigantic as trunks of trees."

I stooped down eagerly and examined the lower jaw-bone of a mastadon and the molars of a dinotherium. "You are right!" I cried. "These mighty animals once lived and died on the shores of this underground sea. Is it possible...oh my God!...that one of these

Bones and Teeth of Mighty Animals

huge monsters may be hidden behind one of these mighty rocks at this very moment?"

I looked around, but nothing alive appeared on these deserted shores.

Even though I had seen many exciting things, I was tired from my recent ordeal and found it necessary to rest, especially if we were going on a sea voyage soon. So we returned to the cave.

The next morning, I awoke completely refreshed. I took a bath in the waters of the sea, had breakfast, and then again walked along the shore with my uncle.

"Where are we now in relation to the surface?" I asked him.

"We are over 1,000 miles from Sneffels and 110 miles under the surface," he said.

"Then that would put us... let's see... somewhere below the Scottish Highlands," I answered.

"You are quite right," he said, laughing.

"Are you now planning to return to the

Taking a Bath in the Sea

surface?" I asked.

"Go back?" he cried. "Before we finish our journey?"

"But we have reached a great sea," I said.

"I judge it to be only about 150 miles across," he replied.

"And how are we to cross it?" I asked with some alarm. "Swim?"

"You shall see," he said.

And I did. Thanks to Hans's hard work, had a raft ten feet long and five feet wide. It was made of fossil wood from the pines and firs that Hans had found and tied together with our sturdy climbing ropes. A mast stood upright, and hanging from it was a sail made from one of our sheets.

At six o'clock on the morning of the 13th of August, we loaded our supplies on the raft and pushed it into the sea. Hans had fashioned a rudder, and he guided us with ease. As the wind was strong, we made good time in the first hours afloat.

Loading Supplies on the Raft

We passed gigantic clumps of seaweed three to four thousand feet long. They looked like snakes stretching beyond the horizon.

After a few hours, Hans baited a hook with a little piece of meat and dropped it into the underground sea. Were there fish in these waters?

We waited a long time, then suddenly Hans pulled up his line. On the hook was a fish, much resembling a lake sturgeon, but of a family that had been extinct for ages—a blind fish that had absolutely no eyes. In this way, we got much-needed food for our future travels.

The second day at sea found the wind steady and the raft moving as quickly as before. We were becoming bored with the trip and impatient to find the other end of the vast sea.

My uncle was scanning the horizon with his telescope, muttering angrily to himself.

"What's wrong, Uncle?" I asked.

"I thought this sea to be only 150 miles

Hans Hooks a Fish.

across, but we have already traveled three times that distance, and we are not nearing any land! I am beginning to wonder if Saknussemm found this sea and crossed it. I wonder if we are still on the right path to the center of the earth."

We sailed on like that for two days more. The only excitement came when, trying to find the depth of the sea, Hans tied a crowbar to a rope and dropped it into the water. It came up half-crushed, with big scratch marks on it.

"What are those marks?" I asked.

Hans looked closely. "Teeth!" he answered.

I decided that I never wanted to see the huge animal with teeth so strong as to crush iron and leave such marks on it.

On Tuesday, the 18th of August, we moved as before. Towards evening, I fell asleep, only to be awakened when the raft was lifted high out of the water.

"What is it?" I yelled.

Hans raised his hand and pointed to a huge

The Crowbar Comes Up Half-Crushed.

black mass moving in and out of the water about 200 yards from the raft.

"A colossal monster!" I cried.

"Yes," cried my uncle, "and over there is a huge sea lizard, and there, closer to the raft, ...a giant crocodile, with teeth at least a foot high! "

Then an enormous whale appeared ... then forty-foot-long turtles and other huge monsters, all heading toward us, ready to destroy our raft with a movement of a tail or a bite of a mouth.

I picked up my rifle, ready to shoot. But Hans stopped me. A bullet would have no effect on the armor scales covering their bodies.

Then, all but two disappeared into the sea. And those two made a rush at one another. One had the head of a lizard, the teeth of a crocodile, and the snout of a porpoise. It was the most fearful of all primitive reptiles—the icthyosaurus, or great fish lizard. The other

Colossal Sea Monsters!

was a monstrous serpent, with the hard shell of a turtle. It was the terrible plesiosaurus, or sea crocodile.

As we watched, the two giants began a furious battle that lasted for hours. Mountains of water dashed over our raft and nearly hurled us headlong into the waves. Hideous hisses from the monsters brought terror to our hearts.

Suddenly the two disappeared beneath tbe waves, almost drawing us into the whirlpool they left behind. Several minutes passed... then the head of the plesiosaurus rose out of the water, its serpent-like neck twisted in the agony of death. Its body convulsed, then stopped. And the mighty snake lay dead on the now calm waters.

As for the icthyosaurus, had he gone under the sea to rest, or would he reappear to destroy us?

A Furious Battle!

A Coming Storm

CHAPTER 10

A Storm at Sea

It was now Friday, the 21st of August. We had traveled more than 800 miles on this sea, and I calculated our position to be exactly under England. The sea was calm, and the fresh wind was moving us along.

Yet, something was different. The clouds, if that is what they could be called, were breaking up into what looked like huge balls of cotton and were falling towards the sea, becoming darker as they fell.

"I think we are in for some sort of storm," I told my uncle.

He pointed up at the sky, but said nothing.

179

It soon became obvious that there was much electricity in the air. My hair started to stand on end, and I think that if one of my companions had touched me, he would have received a terrible shock.

At 10 o'clock, the signs of a storm became even clearer. The clouds were black, and the wind seemed to die down as if getting ready for a battle. The raft sat motionless on the dark sea.

"We should lower the sails," I said.

"No—no," my uncle said angrily. "Let the wind strike us and sweep us away. Perhaps it will finally carry us to the other side of this endless water."

Suddenly the storm hit. It came from all corners of the cavern at once, howling, shrieking, and raging. The darkness increased. The raft rose and fell with the storm, bounding over the waves. My uncle was thrown headlong onto the deck, where he lay quietly. His eyes were open, and he seemed to

The Storm Hits from All Sides.

be enjoying the storm as he held on for his life.

I went to him, crawling so that I would not be tossed overboard into the raging water.

As for Hans, he never moved a muscle. His long hair was blowing wildly in the storm, but he just sat in place.

We were moving at an unbelievable speed before the wind, heading for a curtain of rain.

"Lower the sail! I yelled, using my hand to make a megaphone so that I could be heard above the roaring of the storm.

"No," my uncle yelled back. "Let it alone!"

The sea began to foam wildly. Fearful claps of thunder were accompanied by the brightest lightning I had ever seen. The flashes crossed one another, hurled from every side. Hailstones that shone like lamps struck the raft, threatening to overturn us. My eyes were blinded by the bright flashes in the dark sky. My ears were deafened by the roar of the thunder claps, which were so loud that it seemed as if all the gunpowder in the world

Blinded by Bright Flashes in the Dark Sky

had exploded at the same instant.

The storm did not lessen for even an instant all day and all night, and Sunday, the 23rd, found us still under attack by the elements.

It was Monday, the 24th, and the storm continued as if it had just begun. My uncle and I were broken and tired, but Hans seemed as fresh and alert as the day we had begun our journey, almost two months before.

About 12 o'clock, the storm became worse and we were forced to tie down all of our cargo to the deck of the raft, or else it would have been washed overboard. At times, the entire raft was underwater, and my uncle and I had to tie ourselves to the mast.

I took out my notebook and wrote for my uncle to see: "Take in sail."

He shook his head "yes."

But it was too late. A ball of fire swept over the raft and carried the mast and sail into the sky like a kite.

We were frozen, actually shivering with

The Storm Becomes Worse.

terror. The ball of fire, half-white, half-red moved along, first heading away from our raft then towards it, until finally, it landed on our powder barrel. We knew that an explosion would soon come.

But it did not. The fireball moved again, approaching Hans, then my uncle, then me. Gases coming from it choked us. Suddenly, the ball of fire burst, producing such great electricity that it blinded us all for the moment Then it went out, and darkness once more fell upon the water.

We continued to move rapidly, even though we no longer had a sail. I made some quick calculations. We must have gone under England, the Channel, France, and much of Europe by this time.

Suddenly, there was another great noise—the noise of the sea breaking on a rocky shore. The waves tossed our small craft onto the shore with such force that the raft was wrecked. I would have died had it not been for

A Ball of Fire Lands on the Powder Barrel.

Hans, who carried my broken and bruised body out of the boiling surf and over the slippery rocks that marked the shore.

Our ocean voyage had ended, and I was glad to see the end of the Central Sea.

Hans took my uncle and me and the goods he had managed to save from the wrecked raft to a shelter under a rocky overhang. He prepared some food, but after the last three days, all I wanted to do was sleep.

The next day when I awoke, the weather was again beautiful. Every trace of the storm had disappeared.

"Well, my boy," said my uncle cheerfully, "have you slept soundly?"

"Yes," I replied. "And have we now reached the end of our journey?"

My uncle seemed surprised. "Of course not," he said. "We can now continue on our journey by land to the center of the earth."

"And how will we get back?" I asked.

"Simple," he said with a smile. "When we

Hans Carries Harry out of the Surf.

reach the exact center of the earth, we will simply find a new way back up to the surface or we will follow the way we came."

"And what do we do for provisions?"

"Hans has taken care of that," he said. "He has saved much from the raft, and he will see to it that we find whatever we need along the way. Have you any doubts that he can do what I say?"

I had to admit that Hans could do whatever he set out to do.

We went to the rocky overhang where Hans had laid out the supplies and provisions he had rescued. We had a four-month supply of biscuits, dried fish, and salted meat, plenty of water, and most of our instruments. Only our guns were lost.

"And the raft?" I asked.

"I don't think we'll need it again," said my uncle. "I have an idea that we shall not come out through the same opening by which we entered! "

Hans Lays Out the Provisions He Rescued.

Was my uncle mad?...Little did I know how true his words would prove to be.

"Where do you think we are now in relation to the upper world?" I asked my uncle.

"It is hard to tell exactly, but I calculate that we have traveled about 900 miles upon the sea," he said. "We are about 2,700 miles from Sneffels. That would put us exactly under the Mediterranean Sea."

My uncle took out his compass, as if to prove what he had said. He looked at the needle, and his face went white.

"What's the matter?" I asked.

He could not speak. He closed his eyes, rubbed them, then looked at the needle again.

I took the compass from him and examined it. The needle pointed due north—in the direction we thought was south! There was only one conclusion to be drawn. During the storm, the wind had reversed itself, and the shore on which we now stood was the same one we had left so many days before!

The Compass Reveals a Startling Fact!

"To the Raft!"

CHAPTER 11

A Primitive World

It would be impossible to describe the amazement and rage we felt on finding that we had returned to the shore we had left.

"So," my uncle said grimly, "fate wishes to play tricks with me. Well, I will not retreat."

"Listen, Uncle," I said. "We cannot struggle against that dangerous sea again."

"To the raft!" he cried, as if I hadn't spoken.

Hans began repairing the raft and loading our supplies on board.

"There is no hurry, my boy," said my uncle. "We shall not start until tomorrow. For now, let us explore these shores, for they are somewhat distant from our starting point."

We walked along the sandy shore for a mile, then the sand turned to a dusty material. I was looking at the dust when I felt my uncle halt beside me.

"What's the matter?" I asked, looking up.

But he didn't have to answer. Before my eyes rested the fossil remains of every animal known to man—and some that were undoubtly not yet known. It was more than a scientist could stand.

Suddenly, my uncle's excitement rose, and he darted over the dust to pick up a skull. "Harry, " he cried, "this is a human head! "

I was as amazed and as overjoyed as he. A human skull from this period in history when no human was thought to exist! And a skull covered with a parchment-like skin, with the teeth intact, and with a full head of hair! What wondrous soil was this to have preserved the head for millions of years!

And the body, six feet in length, was there

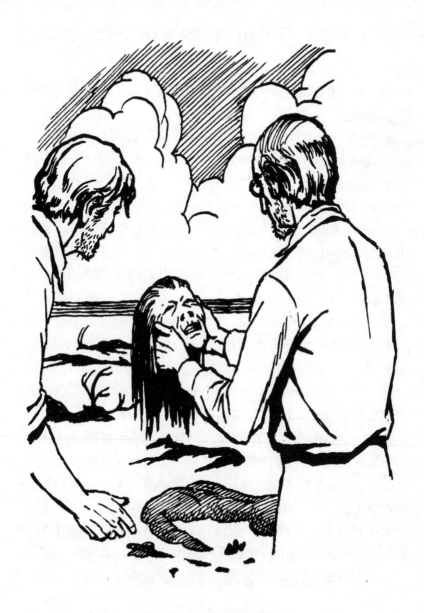

A Human Skull!

too, surrounded by this man's hatchets and flints.

We were in a cemetery of an extinct world! My uncle quickly gathered up many of these specimens to convince the world above. Had these beings been buried by a tremendous earthquake, or had they lived here in this underground world? *And* were any of these men still wandering these shores inside the earth now?

We turned inland towards a vast forest in the distance. We decided to see what new discoveries the forest held for us.

We had just entered the forest and were examining the giant ferns, pines, and yews, when some movement caught my eye. I stopped in my tracks.

There, in the distance, was a herd of mastodons—gigantic elephants of the prehistoric period. They were uprooting trees with their giant trunks and eating them as if they were leaves from a small tree.

A Herd of Gigantic Prehistoric Elephants!

We watched in astonishment.

"Let us get closer," my uncle said.

"No," I answered. "We have no weapons. Come away, I beg you. No man could face these monsters."

"No man?" my uncle whispered. "Then how do you account for him?"

I looked to where my uncle was pointing. There, indeed, was a human being—a gigantic human being—who seemed to be herding the even more gigantic mastodons. He was at least twelve feet tall, with a head as big as a buffalo's. A mane of matted hair covered his gigantic head.

"Come, come!" I cried, dragging my uncle along. "We must get away before he sees us."

For once, my uncle did not resist my suggestion, and fifteen minutes later we were far away from that terrible monster!

When we felt that we were safe from the giant and his monstrous herd, we slowed our pace and headed once more for the Central

A Gigantic Human Herds the Mastadons.

Sea. We were walking along the sandy shore when suddenly, a bright object caught my eye I ran to pick it up.

"What is it?" my uncle asked.

"This," I said, and I handed him a rusty dagger.

"It is only a common knife used by many Icelanders," he said. "It must be Hans's."

"No," I said. "This knife is not a day old, nor a year old, nor a century old, but much more. Yet it is made of steel. Look at the mold and rust on it. I recognize it as a Spanish dagger from the sixteenth century."

"Then some man must have preceded us on this beach," he said. "And the jagged edges on the dagger look as if they were made by someone trying to carve a message on some rock....Perhaps by a man who was trying to indicate the road to the center of the earth!"

We looked at the rocks surrounding the sandy beach and found a narrow path leading from the sea to a cave. We followed it

A Sixteenth-Century Spanish Dagger

carefully, our feet in the water, to a huge over hanging rock. Beneath it lay the entrance to a dark cave.

Inside the cave we found a square slab of granite. On it were carved letters which had been worn by age—the initials of the traveler who had made this journey before us:

"A.S.!" cried my uncle. "You see, I was right. Arne Saknussemm came this way."

Ever since we started our amazing journey, I experienced one surprise after another. But, after finding the initials of Saknussemm here, carved in the bowels of the earth three hundred years ago, I had to admit that now nothing of this journey would be impossible.

"Let us go forward!" I cried eagerly.

But my uncle stopped me. "Let us go back and get Hans," he said. "We will sail the raft to this point on the coast."

Finding Arne Saknussemm's Initials

That evening, we returned to the cave and explored inside. We had gone no more than dozen steps when we were stopped by a huge block of solid granite. There was no turn to take.

"There is no opening here," my uncle said sadly.

"But what about Saknussemm?" I asked.

"Perhaps this rock closed off the passage during the three hundred years since he made his journey," he said.

"We must find a way to remove it! "I cried wildly.

"Perhaps we can attack it with pickaxes and crowbars" my uncle suggested.

"That will never do," I said. "We could never pry it away with ordinary tools. No, we must use gunpowder and blow it out of our way."

"Marvelous!" my uncle cried. "To work!"

By midnight, we had dug a hole in the rock large enough to hold fifty pounds of gun-

Making a Hole in the Rock

powder. We then stretched a long wick to carry the flame to it from outside the cave.

Resisting the temptation to light it immediately, we, instead, slept till morning.

The next day, the 27th of August, we were all up at six o'clock and ready. I took the lantern and went to the fuse, which would take about ten minutes to burn. My uncle and Hans remained in safety on the raft. We planned to sail a distance away to avoid any effects of the explosion.

"Are you ready?" my uncle asked.

"Quite ready," I answered.

"Then fire away!"

My heart was jumping. I lit the wick, then ran back to shore and jumped on the raft, Hans guided us a distance away while the fire was heading for the charge.

"Five minutes," said my uncle,...four... three...two...One minute to go...thirty seconds."...Then the roar of an explosion!

The sea seemed to have gone mad! It

The Roar of an Explosion!

became one huge mountain on top of which tumbled the raft. Then I felt as if we were going down a tremendous well. We clung together in silence.

Beyond the rock which had been blown up, there was a great hole, and the water of the Central Sea poured into it like a mighty torrent, forming an inland sea and dragging us along with it!

For two hours, the raft moved down this sea, achieving speeds of over a hundred miles per hour. We held onto each other lest we fall off the raft and be killed.

There was no doubt that we were upon the road taken by Saknussemm, but instead of climbing down as we had planned, we were taking the whole sea with us.

After several hours, the tunnel widened, but the raft kept spinning and rushing at lightning speed—more than a hundred miles an hour.

I managed to recover my balance enough to check our supplies. Most had disappeared! Of

The Sea Pours into a Great Hole.

all our instruments, only the chronometer and the compass were on the raft. And to make things even worse, no food—not even one day's supply—remained!

Suddenly, I felt a shock, yet we did not hit anything hard. Water poured all over us. We were caught under a giant waterfall, which almost drowned us. But in a few seconds, the raft was forced out from under it, and we were once more along our way.

"Harry, Harry," I heard my uncle call. "Do you see what has happened? We are now being carried upward."

I touched the wall, which ripped at my hand. We were indeed going upward, and at an extraordinary speed!

"The water of the Central Sea must have hit the bottom," my uncle reasoned, "and it is now forcing us up this narrow well."

A whole hour passed. The fate that awaited us seemed to be a rock roof at the top of the well...and a crushing death!

Caught Under a Giant Waterfall

Rising at an Alarming Rate of Speed

CHAPTER 12

A Volcano Erupts

We continued to rise at an alarming rate of speed. I was frightened of what was to come. My uncle must have seen the look of fear upon my face.

"While there is life, there is hope," he said. "Let us eat something to keep up our strength."

Hans shook his head sadly.

"What!" yelled my uncle. "Do you mean to say that all of our provisions are lost?"

"Yes," I answered. Then I dropped into a kind of trance, dreaming about my youth and my home and Gretchen and the food we had left behind.

When I awoke from my trance, I could feel a new sensation. The temperature was rising rapidly as our raft. I could not tell what the temperature was exactly, but I would guess that it had reached at least 120 degrees. "Why the change in temperature?" I wondered.

"If we are not drowned or smashed flat like pancakes, we shall be burned alive," I said aloud.

My uncle just shrugged his shoulders and looked upward. "I still have hope," he said coolly.

Hours passed in this manner. And as we progressed upward, the temperature rose with us. I began to feel as if we were bathed in hot and burning air. Never before had I felt anything like it. We began to take off our clothing, the slightest shirt or undershirt being extremely uncomfortable.

"Are we ascending into a living fire?" I cried,

Bathed in Hot and Burning Air

when the heat became greater.

"No, no, it is impossible," he said, knowing, however, that nothing on this journey was an impossibility.

"And yet," I answered, "the walls of the tunnel are red hot. And listen, do you hear those thunderous explosions?"

An idea seemed to strike my uncle, and I could see his mind wrestling with it.

"Uncle! " I cried. "We are lost. We must be caught in a earthquake. The walls around us are cracking! The water beneath us is boiling!"

"You are wrong," he answered. "Very wrong."

"What do you mean?" I cried.

"This is more than an earthquake, Harry. Something more important by far. It is an eruption!"

"An eruption?" I gasped. "Then we are in a volcanic shaft of a crater that is getting ready to erupt?"

"The Walls of the Tunnel Are Red Hot."

"Yes," he answered with a smile on his face "And this is one of the best things that could have happened to us."

"What!" I screamed. "Have you gone mad? We are in a well of burning and boiling lava We are about to be spit out of the earth, along with whirlwinds of flame and huge rocks, and you say this is the best..."

"Don't you see, Harry?" he said calmly. "This is our only chance of escaping from the interior of the earth and seeing the light of day."

I suddenly realized that my uncle was right.

We passed the whole night rapidly going up through the burning tunnel. Under the raft was a mass of boiling water, and under that, a heaving mass of lava and rocks.

I found myself wondering what mountain we were climbing at such speed, and on what part of the world we would be shot out... As if it really mattered... for there was no escape!

Soon, a dim light reached us from above. To

Going Up Through the Burning Tunnel

the right and left I could make out long dark hallways of rock from which awful smoke and horrible sulphur gases poured out. Tongues of fire, sparkling and crackling, appeared about to lick us up. The hour had come!

"Look, Uncle, look!" I cried.

"Don't worry," he said. "The tunnel is widening. It shall soon be over."

The temperature had reached 200 degrees, and sweat rushed from every pore in our bodies. Only the speed of our travel kept us from stifling to death.

About eight o'clock in the morning, the ascent of the raft stopped completely. We moved neither upward nor fell back into the earth.

"The eruption has failed! " I cried. "We shall never reach the surface."

"Do not worry," my uncle said. "The nature of eruptions is such that they move in stages. We will begin our ascent again in ten minutes."

Horrible Sulphur Gases Pour Out.

And he was correct to the minute.

Soon, the raft began to move again. The heat was now unbearable. I looked forward to being thrown from the crater onto the snowy slopes of some volcano in the North Country. The snow, ice, and cold would be a welcome reliel from the heat of the shaft in which we now traveled.

This stopping and starting occurred many times during those hours. I don't remember much of what came next. What I do remember is a mass of rocks moving upward, numerous explosions, and the raft going round and round like a spinning top as it floated on a stream of hot lava, amidst a falling cloud of ashes.

The last thing I saw was the figure of Hans appearing to be surrounded by the halo of a burning blaze. Then I felt a sensation like a man being shot from the mouth of a cannon with his body flying into empty space!

Shot from the Mouth of a Cannon!

Returned to Earth on a Mountain Slope

CHAPTER 13

The Journey Ends

When I opened my eyes, I felt Hans clutching me firmly by my belt. With his other hand, he held my uncle. I was not badly wounded, but bruised all over my body.

After a moment, I looked around. I was lying down on the slope of a mountain, not two yards from a cliff over which I would have fallen if Hans had not saved me.

"Where are we?" asked my uncle, who seemed unhappy at having returned to earth.

Hans shrugged his shoulders.

"Are we in Iceland?" I asked Hans.

227

"No," he said.

"You must be wrong," my uncle cried.

But Hans was not wrong. Instead of the glaciers and snow of Iceland, which I had expected to see, I found myself on a mountain that was baked by the burning sun.

"It really does not look like Iceland," my uncle observed. "Look down the mountain. There are green trees, among them fig and olive trees. And beyond that, a little port with houses and fishing boats. No, we are not anywhere near the Arctic region from which we began. Let us walk down the mountain and see if we can find food and water."

After two hours of walking, a beautiful country spread out before us, with olives, pomegranites, and grapes growing wild. We ate our fill and drank from a spring of fresh water.

While we were eating, a young, poorly dressed child appeared between two olive trees.

Nowhere Near the Arctic Region

"Ah!" I cried. "An inhabitant of this country. Perhaps we can find out where we are."

The young boy was terribly frightened at seeing three half-naked men, with tangled and ragged beards, eating like savages.

My uncle spoke softly in German. "What is the name of this mountain, my boy?"

There was no answer.

"Good," said my uncle. "We are not in Germany."

He asked the question again, this time in English.

Again, there was no answer.

My uncle asked again, this time in French.

The young boy shook his head to indicate that he did not understand.

"I will try him in Italian," my uncle said *"Come si noma questa isola?"*—What is the name of this island?

"Stromboli," the boy answered quickly, then turned and dashed away, disappearing quickly

The Young Boy Does Not Understand.

in the olive groves.

"Stromboli!" I cried. "We have come to the surface in the center of the Mediterranean. Stromboli! Stromboli! And the mighty volcano we came up through is the fierce and famous Mount Etna!"

Ah—what a journey! What a marvelous and extraordinary journey! We had entered the earth by one volcano and had come out by another. And Etna was at least 3,600 miles from Sneffels. We had left the snows of Iceland and returned under the sun on the island of Stromboli.

We continued our journey down to the little port. We passed ourselves off as shipwrecked travelers, for had the superstitious people of this island known the truth, they would have called us demons from Hell!

The Fierce and Famous Mount Etna!

Leaving Stromboli

CHAPTER 14

Home Again

We were taken in by the Stromboli fishermen, who gave us clothes and food. And forty-eight hours later, on the 30th of September, a boat took us to the city of Messina on Sicily.

On Friday, the 4th of October, we left for France, and reached Hamburg, Germany, on the 9th of October.

Thanks to the gossipy tongue of Martha, my uncle's housekeeper, the word of our trip had spread throughout Hamburg and then all over the world. Upon hearing that we had attempted a journey to the center of the earth, most people believed that we would never again be seen. Then, when they saw us home safely, they believed it even less.

But the prescence of Hans and the stray scraps of information we presented soon changed their minds. My uncle became a great man, and I became the nephew of a great man.... and something of a hero myself.

Hamburg gave a festival in our honor, which my uncle related all the details of our incredible trip.

That same day, he deposited the parchment left by Arne Saknussemm in the town library He expressed his regrets that he could not follow the route of the Icelander all the way to the center of the earth. He was modest in glory, but his reputation only increased.

When Hans decided to leave Hamburg for his beloved home in Iceland, my uncle and I were both saddened. We will never forget the brave and trusted guide who had saved lives many times.

A Festival in Hamburg

To conclude, I must say that our journey into the interior of the earth created great excitement throughout the world, and our story was published in many languages.

During his lifetime, my uncle enjoyed all the glory he deserved.

As for me, I married Gretchen and moved into my own house near my uncle's. There, I continued to work with the distinguished professor for the rest of his days.

Uncle and Nephew Continue Their Work.

Collect the complete series of

GREAT ILLUSTRATED CLASSICS
The series treasured by generations of readers of all ages!
Available from Waldman Publishing

1. Around the World in 80 Days
2. Black Beauty
3. The Call of the Wild
4. Little Women
5. Oliver Twist
6. The Adventures of Tom Sawyer
7. Treasure Island
8. The Wizard of Oz
9. A Journey to the Center of the Earth
10. The Strange Case of Dr. Jekyll and Mr. Hyde
11. Swiss Family Robinson
12. Heidi
13. The Merry Adventures of Robin Hood
14. The Adventures of Huckleberry Finn
15. The Three Musketeers
16. Moby Dick
17. The Adventures of Robinson Crusoe
18. 20,000 Leagues Under the Sea
19. The Mutiny on the Bounty
20. Kidnapped
21. Great Expectations
22. The Prince and the Pauper
23. David Copperfield
24. The Last of the Mohicans
25. The Adventures of Sherlock Holmes
26. A Tale of Two Cities
27. The Red Badge of Courage
28. The Count of Monte Cristo
29. Captains Courageous
30. Frankenstein
31. King Arthur and The Knights of the Round Table
32. The Time Machine
33. Tales of Mystery and Terror
34. White Fang
35. Ivanhoe
36. The Hunchback of Notre Dame
37. The Jungle Book
38. The Secret Garden
39. The Wind in the Willows
40. Hans Brinker
41. Gulliver's Travels
42. Anne of Green Gables
43. Pollyanna
44. The Invisible Man
45. The Legend of Sleepy Hollow and Rip Van Winkle
46. Peter Pan
47. The Picture of Dorian Gray
48. Rebecca of Sunnybrook Farm
49. Grimm's Fairy Tales
50. Alice in Wonderland
51. Dracula
52. Pride and Prejudice
53. The War of the Worlds
54. King Solomon's Mines
55. Snow White and Other Stories
56. Beauty & The Beast and Other Stories
57. Cinderella and Other Stories
58. The Little Mermaid and Other Stories
59. Sleeping Beauty and Other Stories
60. Aesop's Fables
61. Jane Eyre
62. The Phantom of the Opera
63. The House of the Seven Gables
64. The Man in the Iron Mask
65. Sherlock Holmes and the Case of The Hound of the Baskervilles
66. A Little Princess

And for the holidays and special occasions
1. A Christmas Carol   2. Christmas Bedtime Stories
3. Stories from the Bible

Try these exciting titles in the

GREAT AMERICAN HEROES SERIES

1. Daniel Boone
2. Benjamin Franklin
3. George Washington
4. Babe Ruth
5. Eleanor Roosevelt
6. Clara Barton
7. Martin Luther King
8. Jackie Robinson

Find our books at Michaels Arts and Crafts,
or call us at (212) 730-9590 or email us at info@waldmanbooks.com
Visit us at http//:www.waldmanbooks.com